Moonflower

Words that are alive under the evening stars

Arya Ravindra Ugale

BookLeaf Publishing

India | USA | UK

Dedication

To the dreamers who find beauty in the shadows,
To the believers who hold on when the light feels dim,
To the hearts that have loved, lost, and dared to love
again— This book is for you.
And to the moonflower within us all,
Blooming quietly in the dark,
May you always find the courage to rise,
To begin anew, and to never stop hoping.
To life, love and hope.

Preface

Life, in all its intricacies, is a journey—a tapestry woven from threads of joy and sorrow, love and loss, beginnings and endings. *Moonflower* is not merely a collection of poems; it is a story, a chronicle of the human spirit navigating through the labyrinth of existence.

This book invites you to walk alongside its verses, tracing the path of life's milestones: the innocence of birth, the tempest of youth, the weight of responsibility, the beauty of love, the bonds of friendship, and the pangs of heartbreak. Each poem is a mirror reflecting the many faces of our shared humanity, tied together by an unyielding thread of hope.

The final piece, "Moonflower," serves as a beacon—a reminder that even in the depths of despair, the seed of renewal lies dormant, waiting to bloom. Just as the moonflower unfurls under the cover of night, hope and love persist, guiding us toward a new dawn. Even when life feels fragile or fleeting, love never truly fades; it remains, a quiet yet powerful force, lighting the way. *Moonflower* is for anyone seeking solace, strength, and a gentle reminder that the night always gives way to day. May these poems resonate with your heart and inspire you to embrace the enduring beauty of life's cycle.

Acknowledgements

This book would not have been possible without the unwavering support, inspiration, and encouragement of many remarkable souls.

To my family, thank you for believing in me, for your endless love, and for nurturing my dreams even when they seemed far-fetched. Your support has been my anchor.

To my friends, thank you for the laughter, the understanding, and the moments that have shaped these pages. You've been the light in my darkest hours.

To the readers who find meaning in these words, thank you for allowing *Moonflower* to bloom in your hands and hearts. Your presence gives life to these poems.

Finally, to life itself—its trials, triumphs, and transitions— for gifting me the emotions, stories. Grateful for everything and Thankful to everyone.

1. Daffodil

Beginning of spring with floral sights,
A fresh bloom of warmth ignites.

First light of sun on the winter worn soul,
Birth of daffodils greets the world, bright and whole.
Blooming of hope in a melting heart,
As winter winds swirl and depart,
Air of floral spring
Turning life's first breath into art.

As the chirping of birds in spring,
Life's first cry is waiting to sing.
New life awakens, soft and divine,
As meadow of daffodils brightly shine.

As New-born life brings gentle light,
Bundles of joy and a smile takes flight.
Just as daffodils intertwine,
A harmony of hope divine.

Moving ahead with dreams that bind,
Through the fields of floral kind,
Where life and blossoms softly align.

2. Bluebell

Bluebells sway in the woods,
where laughter hides in quiet moods.
Questions bloom like tender buds,
Curiosities weaving through the hush of woods.

Tall trees rise in forest deep,
she is small and innocent in shadows sleep.
Awed by vastness of world around,
Bluebells rest in comfort found.

Shy yet magical ,her bloom,
Surprising the woods with sweet perfume.

Mischief lingers, softly forbidden,
Beneath the shadows, burdens hidden.
Backs bend low beneath the strain,
Yet she blooms through joy and pain.

3. Daisy

Weaving dreams in fields of endless sun,
Daisies dance as their joy has just begun.
Carefree, barefoot, a soul takes its stand,
A heart of purity, like daisies in the land.

As a sunflower misunderstood by few,
it is little daisy's dew.
A lone daisy stiving to belong,
In the meadow of view
Yet blooming in fields strong.

Shiny in the golden breeze,
She is tiny amongst the tall trees.
Our daisy is weaving dreams,
A day will bring the gleams.

Laughter is all she brings,
Day and night her petals sing.
Intwined in the power of breeze,
All that she needs to fly is, wings.

4. Sunflower

Rising tall in the sky reaching for light,
there is a sunflower in sight.
Unfolding the dreams of childhood,
She is sunflower still,
Rising tall in the sky reaching for light.

Across the fields the beauty is serene,
Mighty blossom dreaming for the reign.
She is sunflower still,
Rising tall in the sky reaching for light.

Aspirations in sight, she is shining bright,
She is sunflower still,
Rising tall in the sky with his own will.

With her lofty brilliance,
And radiant shine,
There is stopping for the horizon,
As she is sunflower still,
Rising tall in the sky reaching for light.

5. Lavender

Lavender's silence is heard around,
she is struggling to be found.
Swaying with the rest,
she is on her own quest.

On the fields with other is her nest,
But together yet alone,
she is not like the rest,
she can see her throne,
But the road to that is yet unknown.

Bustling through the winds,
Living the same kinds.
Cluster is always admired as bind,
Lone is not beauty to find.

It is only time to define,
For what is to refine.
Together is what can unwind,
A lone lavender is not of her kind.

6. Tulip

Love's first blush painted on her petals,
Heart is where her beauty settles.
Season of love and blossom of spring,
Rhythms of love birds sing.

White, red, yellow, pink,
Glimpses of beauty not to blink.
Love's first blush painted on her petals,
she is tulip, between mind and heart she meddles.

Gentle blossoming of spring love,
Tulip finds the first, just as turtle dove.
Love's first blush painted on her petals,
she is tulip, Binding hearts with unseen metals.

Search of warmth completes here,
Tulip along the side of love, cheers.
Love's first blush painted on her petals,
Binding hearts with unseen metals.

7. Freesia

Freesia dances in harmony,
With fragrance of hope to many.
Loyalty of togetherness stand still,
And yet she remains lone still.

She is there for others,
Whilst others giving up on her,
Just as the season of fall ponders,
And every other leaf wanders.

Promises to never break,
She trusts the bond,
Only to make her heart ache,
She promises still and beyond.

She believes, Fall is only till dawn,
As she makes the bond beyond.
She grows with faith and hope,
To swallow every promise she wrote.

8. Iris

Iris stands still with pride,
As the winter winds slide.
She firms her faith,
As spring awaits, with open gates.

Winter's old foliage gusting away,
Iris grows in the sunny spring day.
There awaits her journey,
Along with spring as her attorney.

She dances with faith,
As her tour of life waits.
she creates her novelty,
Without inflecting her loyalty,
There awaits her journey.

Her strength and belief,
Only needs sunny relief.
There awaits her journey,
Along with spring as her attorney.

9. Forget-me-not

Blue Sky around and sun in center,
Forget-me-not blooms as sun enters.

She blooms in the heart's garden,
preserving the echoes of a joyful past,
Mistakes made should be forgotten,
Song of the past, will have the verse that last

The past of memories,
Crying in worries,
Shouting — forget-me-not,
Promising to soon meet in the same spot.

With the joy fading away,
She still dances in sway.
After every day,
Only memories stay.

10. Chrysanthemum

Mums bloom with passion,
embers of ambition lighting the way,
Her calm and soothing patience
Compels our eyes to obey.

Strongest desire she proclaim,
As her vibrant hues exclaim a flame.
Winds howl and skies weep,
Yet mums unbowed with roots deep.

She teaches hearts that seek sun,
The fight for light has just begun.
Through stormy and fleeting days,
She whispers hope in golden rays.

Each of her tells a tale of fire,
Of passion, of heart's desire.
No fleeting storm can dim her glow,
Her strength will always show.

11. Camelia

Camelia's soft petals, in perfect grace,
A pure heart, a warm embrace.
With time, her bloom reveals,
The quite depth that true love feels.

Her gentle hues paint the skies,
Just like a tale captured in lover's eyes.
Where words are not suffice,
Camelia speaks in whisper twice.

Each petal a promise, each shade a dream,
Love is a tender bond, a flowing stream.
No storm can harm, no tear can sever,
Her love that blooms is forever.

Through every storm, she will endure,
Her love so boundless, so pure.
Never so alive, felt her heart,
That is just true love's art.

12. Peony

Peony tells a tale, in her vibrant bloom,
Of efforts bold, that never gloom.
Each fold, each hue a sign,
Of hope and dreams divine.

She sways with regal air,
With her bright shine, beyond compare.
She whispers hope in streams,
With a garden of her cherished dreams.

Even with a sigh,
Her crown is held high.
With joy that stays,
And a life in endless praise.

Blooms of sorrows renew,
With her vibrant blush and morning dew.
Flourishing with her roots held tight,
She is a symbol of life's delight.

13. Gardenia

Gardenia's fragrance whispers soft and true,
Of hidden worlds and shadow's hue.
A bloom so pure and wide,
A universe of dreams inside.

Quiet nights where her story sleeps,
In fragrant folds, memories she keeps.
A bloom so pure and wide,
A universe of dreams inside.

She guards the heart, with depth under,
All her own ,a world of wonder.
A bloom so pure and wide,
A universe of dreams inside.

Despite the odds, her beauty grows,
Like a mirror which beauty shows.
A bloom so pure and wide,
A universe of dreams inside.

14. Carnation

In the howling wind,
Carnation calms the mind.
Storms violently break,
But her bloom will never quake.

Though trials fail, and shadows fall,
Her bloom persists, defying all.
Each of her petal whispers to be true,
The strength you seek resides in you.

Her charm grows through earth's torn,
From pain, a greater strength is born.
In fields once scorched, she lifts her face,
With a sigh of hope and grace.

Her roots deep with spirit wide,
Her courage, unbent by tide.
Each of her petal whispers to be true,
The strength you seek resides in you.

15. Orchid

Orchid's bloom, a timeless heart,
With her hues in wisdom's art.
Stem of work, a woven thread,
Thoughts once confused , now widespread.

With strength, she softly grows,
As a beauty what all knows.
She stands composed as a work refined,
She blooms with heart and mind.

Each petal hides a story true,
Her beauty is all what we knew.
Her pain speaks of past,
With wisdom earned and beauty to last.

Her sorrows are nowhere to trace,
As they got replaced with hope and grace.
In shadows, she finds her place,
Her strength is all to embrace.

16. Hydrangea

Hydrangea's bloom , a gentle guide,
To hold life's treasures deep inside.
With shifting hues, she shows the way,
To cherish light every day.

Through each cluster, a story blooms,
Of fears faced and quiet rooms.
She bends and yet still thrives,
A symbol of grateful, steadfast lives.

Each petal speaks moments of past,
Through cluster of shadows cast.
Her colors changes with grace,
Her place being a sacred space.

Each bloom holds a whispered prayer,
Thanking all who brought her here.
With shifting hues, she shows the way,
To cherish light every day.

17. Ranunculus

In golden rays, buttercup spins her light,
A sense of joy, a pure delight.
Every petal sings a song,
Tunes playing where they belong.

Each fold reveals a world of cheer,
A smile with a memory dear.
Her glance, a gift so sweet,
Her smile makes the heart complete.

Her beauty is so fine,
A token of life's grand design.
Fragrance as calm and kind,
Where hope and grace bind.

Hues glow with radiant flow,
Upon her sunlight bestow.
Dancing along the wind,
Her joy is every where to find.

18. Hibiscus

A vivid bloom as the day begun,
Hibiscus's hues claim the sun.
Bright and clear as gets the sky,
Her beauty one cannot defy.

Her petals wide, a fiery call,
To seize the moment, gives her all.
With every bloom, a lesson clear,
To live with zeal, to hold life near.

She blooms bold and free,
Her strength shapes her destiny.
Her vibrant heart beats with the breeze,
A song of life sung through the trees.

She fears no one, bows to none,
She sparks with fun.
Her bloom, burst of fire,
Ignites the soul with pure desire.

19. Rose

In fiery red or purest white,
Rose shines in love day and night.
In vibrant blooms, she softly sighs,
A love that lives, that never dies.

Known by all, a symbol of love,
Her sight is so, one cannot unlove.
Her thorns speak,
Of passion strong that hearts seek.

Her colors may fade,
Yet her presence is prayed.
Song of love quietly plays,
As heart yearns to stay.

She is a vow of joy and pain,
Yet dances with soothing rain.
She declares with gentle grace,
True love endures in every space.

20. Anemone

In fleeting bloom, anemone softy shows,
The grace in change, the peace she knows.
She sways with winds so free,
A quiet dance with destiny.

Petals weak and yet she thrives,
A symbol of resilient lives.
Her sight calm and true,
Reminder for life to begin new.

Her beauty speaks for sight unknown,
With many and yet alone.
Shades of rebirth with tender joy,
New cannot have question why.

Through wind howling, skies unknown,
Her roots, her strength is shown.
She blooms with quite grace,
With gentle light, hope to embrace.

21. Moonflower

In silent noise of night moonflower wakes,
A bloom that only starlight takes.
Petals glow in flame,
A spark in twilight's frame.

A fragile time of song's release,
She sings in endless peace.
Under the moon's silver gaze,
Her beauty always amaze.

Each petal holds memory pure,
Love in every corner that can cure.
Each fold makes heart to lure,
Soon fades and yet endless for sure.

At night she lifts her face,
With all that beauty and grace,
She blooms, then fades away,
Yet whispers, 'Love will always stay.

www.ingramcontent.com/pod-product-compliance
Lightning Source LLC
LaVergne TN
LVHW021350200726
843509LV00014B/2776